So I Looked Down to Camelot

Rosamund Stanhope, *So I Looked Down to Camelot*. Flood Editions.

So I Looked Down to Camelot

The Greenhouse

Seeing December's filicale,
   Her nervous woods,
In the red sound of the soil
I plot my trowel,
   Looking for round green words.

Plants creep and spire,
   Leaves coil and trace
   Their potted artifice.
In the red sound of the air
The heart's forced temperature
Heats the induced flower.

Far from the glass house
Constrained and aphyllous
   The leaves have shot their songs
   With brown and withered tongues.

And here I plot my trowel

Fearing no less

Such orchid skill,

Such anode emptiness.

So I Looked Down to Camelot

So I looked down to Camelot,
 Watching all Tuesday up and down the fog.
 The strip-mill thumped, the blind man with his dog
Stared February out,
And Jim in his new coat
 Whistled his marriage vow.

 I heard the hooter blow.
A hearse with wreaths and relatives
And tears and gloves
 Went by,
 The 'busman and the neighbour's boy,
 The fitter on a job.

 I tore the page!
The mirror cracked from edge to edge,
 I saw the new sky grow
 And reached the kerb

And built my boat
And laughed my name, and died.

And quick as life they ran,
The neighbour's boy, the dustbin man
And Jim in his new coat.

The Loud-Leaved Trees

The loud-leaved trees
    Having a shape and summer face
    Can dogmatise
In virid images.

Using this green prerogative
    Of metaphor and may
    They have their integrated say
Serrate as elm, entire as love.

But when the whisper of the year,
    That paper colloquy,
    Poses the fall July
Can hear,

Logic interrogates the bough,
    Concept invades the scar,
    Abstraction shakes the sycamore
And, colourless as snow,

Winter philosophies concede
    What in the thought-shaped twigs the spider mends,
Fragile as filicale and spare as need—
    A lace intelligence.

So the Expensive Sun

So the expensive sun
Coins green, spends June,
   In opulent summer pours
   On rich, cosmetic flowers
Its largesse and its lien.

So the expensive spring
   Hands the year out
   And in a fresh, extravagant coat
Mints thrum, pays song.

So the expensive heart
   Where no deciduous mood contains
   December in the sense
Making no counterfeit
   Wears silver in the veins;
Bears with a capital delight

The twelvemonth trees

Making the round year start

In all its orchard affluence,

The shooting heart her green artilleries.

Cinderella

Hoping for parties and a prince
The clock, the dresser and the hanging spoons,
   The pulley and the larder wear
   Too much their serviceable gear.
   And then—the holiday footstep on the stair!

Yes. The expensive wand,
Like August in the office land,
Makes castles out of sand.
   The pumpkin and the mouse,
The black rat at the cheddar rind,
   The home-made dress
Become the coach, the four-in-hand,
   The lawn, the lace.

And then, let midnight strike,
   The slipper drop,
   Let the joy fly, the party stop,

The story end on its fake.
In palace and in princess ways
The magic stays.

The faggots and the dishes tower
Like castles in the Spanish air,
The pumpkin gilds the shelf,
The gay mice laugh,
Horses are horses, rats are rats
As clever as their whiskered wits,
And all the kitchen moments chime
Louder than princes, longer than a dream.

The Three Travellers

I, Caspar, built my crown
From Shiraz up to Hamadan.
   The desert blossomed gold
   And kings smiled in the shaping world.
From Baghdad to the coast
   The cobbled rock, the shrinking sand
   Made flint and whirlpool of the land.
The star looked iron in the West.

My censers bloomed and shone
From Meshed out to Babylon,
   My hanging walls of air
   Breathed God into a star.
Until the sewage of the Nile,
The camel dung, the fodder bile
   Blew from the manger stalls
   The stench of living animals.

I, medicined with myrrh,
From Basra and the hot bazaar
    Humped down the thieves' highway
    All in the jolting day.
Then, toiling up the crosswise hill,
I came upon the skull,
    And lovely in the listless feet
    The wide wounds beat.

The Light Puts Out the Conifer

The light puts out the conifer,
Rooms in the bookcase air.
June eyes must draw
Their summers on the street
When leaves fall in the chapter of the year.

Blinds blot the stoic bough,
The footnight snow.
Warm granaries
Hoard their Julys
By that synthetic sun, the grate.

Bring in the Christmas tree!
Make up the ghost,
The conifer, the Christ,
With tinsel and with tea.
Wrap that old yew, the brain,
The dustbin man,

In coloured rain,

A bright, cosmetic tale.

Plant out the gall.

Chant in the talk, the toast,

The cardboard host,

The paper Bethlehems.

Such soil redeems

The squat, unstable root,

Lights hide the winding-sheet,

Stars mask the grave,

Toys insulate

The real delight, the difficult love.

The Window on the Stairs

And since the garden eyes have grown
One side for looking at the sun
    Such a stair gaze confirms
    The sun moves as it warms.

And since a street heart knows
One way of looking from the house
    Such a step watch may prove
    The chambers of a further love.

The pine end post
That sees from east to west,
    Before and after,
    The front room manners, back room laughter,

Takes out the lock from the eye
Where stairs can turn without a key,
    Having the here and there
    The traffic and the pergola

Unroomed by the broadside gaze
Of unpartitioned days
  Whose fenceless windows build
  Large ways of looking at the world.

Bartimeus

There the suede noises
    The sounds of silk and shame
    Are faith and form.
The small town passes,
    The small years chime.

But water-dark and down
    The sounding stair
    The ideas are
    Lit by no door
No window-pane
Where hearings drown.

The hand behind the love
    The hat behind the grace
Behave like trees and move
    And have three ways
    And quench all noise.

What the rain preaches
    What the stars say
    Vanish in the gold eye
    The wet day
Like God among the churches.

That Summer Paragon

That summer paragon
The prelate corn
That preaches in the sun
That gowns in green
Earns blame nor benison.

That August baronet
The velvet fruit
That boughs no blight
That pours no purple out
Gains salt nor shoot.

That marred and milled for bread
    That spoiled for wine
That ripe and ready-made
    October man
Knows autumn in the bud
    Sows vintage in the vein
Grows leaven in the pride.

A Resonant Idea

A resonant idea
    That struck my speech
        In the middle of the head
Put minutes in my ear
    Made my mouth watch
        Like birds among the dead.

As Wednesday as the world
    In the centre of the work
    Where April like a clerk
        Went writing by
        From Monday till July
    The days turned in the dark
Like thoughts among the old

    And watched the clock
From nine till summerhood
    And minutes were

A Saturday affair
And love was after church
And after love was lunch
Till August struck.

But then the chime
Of here till season time
Went ringing into sound
The whole ear round
So that I stood
From January on to bed
And earned the time I wound
And heard the time I had.

Cautionary Tale

Out by the weather once
    He sat to spin
    When all the winds were green
    Or as the ways came in
      Loud with a long March,
Wide as a dunce
    Drew fortune with a pin
      Thumbing the years with the birch,
    Looking out like a caravan
    On birds and men.

A son he had,
A likely lad,
Who learnt his tables and his head
And went from worse to bad,
    From bad to good
    Out of the quiet, illiterate wood;
      Shot through the educable air

And knew what dials and handles were,
Till, clever enough for war,
Where that one sat and read
His leaves in the long shade
He made his bed
And lay upon his bier.

The Diocese of Snow

The diocese of snow
Her absolute gives now
    Easing the difficult town
    Where white waits like a noun.
Verbiage of the minster
Doctrine and dissenter
Have their one white answer.

Have their one white flower
Burdock and provender
Barley and tare,
    Bootprint and footstep down
    Will sculpture out the man
    Where the form goes alone.

Fields fine to stall and stack
When adjectives come back.
Fallow and brake,

Parenthesis, degree,
Clause and diversity
Parish in the eye.

And house and house
When the snow disappears
Their disparate shires retrace,
Coloured and various;
Burdock and yield,
Footpad and hypocrite and scold
Anomalous and dear
For the choice of the share
When the white priests thaw
On the lay and intricate world.

A River-Looking Man

A river-looking man
   As April as the sedge
   Came and sat in my hedge
     And fished the morning by.

Did he rake his coil with a pin?
     Did he silk his line with a fly?
Did he grub the tiddlers in
   Or coax the singular bream?

I do not know, but he was
   By the morning and minute stream
     As trout and minnow are
     Dragonfly and dor
     Salmon-creel and jar

Expensive as the sun
That buys the exquisite grass
    Where the reel and float of time
    Bait on the drink of a dream.

The Park Named Hitherto

The park named Hitherto
   Where former trees
      Stars and adventures hang
   And ageless boys
      Play at the year and sing
In the satisfactory snow
Was never now.

Seen through an open wish
   That never closed on grass
      The viaduct is far
From the knocking rails and the slush
      Where stars and adventures are
   But the road never was.

I clang by its plot and out
   To the system of the town
      Where the boring traffic goes

And the only adventure is

The hair on the ruined coat

  Or the possible sun.

And boys and trees and all

  Spin by the wheels of place

  To a snowless Samothrace

  As the brick builds on

To the risks of weathers that really fall

  When the sky breaks down

  And the worlds of the town.

Littoral

Crowfoot and heal
Borage and the spontaneous kale
    Start from the sea
Their unpremeditated shell,
      Where, though the season's tend,
      Whiter than marram in the wind
    They borrow day,
    Catch life and, in the eye
    Of each Hephaestus passing by,
Love that is not reciprocal.

As mind could make,
Eclectic in its work,
    A Cytheraean cosmos of
    Achilous love,
Ironware and rack,
      Cast Calibans of shards

And all the corrugated frauds

That conscious love affords

Lump on the shore

Their liveries of knowledge and power.

Miniature Snowstorm

Yore years and airs snow on
Their timeless eiderdown
    From nursery galleries,
    And through the glass of eyes
    Plucked geese like sheep are woolled
To the ascending child.

There streets as white as lint
Make soft all argument,
    Make void all difference;
    Footprints of once
Become the chart of now
In sugarloafing snow.

Footsteps which stood
In unclocked winterhood
    Are out and in the room

Where thoughts can tick and time
The way they wound,
Now snow is out of sound.

Now snow is out of heart,
An intellect apart,
    Now geese are rain grown cold
    And flocks dispelled
A face to face ago,
I tip the globe and know
    The hand that tilts the world,
    The thought that darks the child.

In Praise of
Living Civilisations

My flesh and taxi love,
  You need no Corinth sky
  To arch mythology,
    No Attic attitude
Supports your architrave.
  You hug a living boy
    And hear him bleed.

No marble sweats your lust,
  No Florentine repair
Could chisel out of dust
  Your capitals in air.
  Warm fingers build your hair,
Warm hands discuss your waist.

Then stretch your dead! and go
  Where cities quick with noise

On columns black with news
    Hang out the washday year
Parisian as now
    With pediments of here;
Where Londons of delight
Rock in the pointed night.

Persons from Porlock

Meals to be plied, fires to be bought,
You with your business at the hand
Talking away my thought
Where opium wined and dined,
How small you beer the mind!

How your clerk ways abolish
With a blue lead the murex hours,
How copy out in chores
The inimitable furniture, demolish
The castles in my airs!
I would shake out my casuistry, polish
My syntax, dust the chemistry of stars
To hitch my dactyls, darn
Achilles, turn a sheet of metaphors.

I talk in tons; you have me caught
To quibble at the figure of an ounce,

You comma in the general sense,

You dot above the art!

Then cross my needs and go,

Doffing your chat at the gate,

Taking your leave with well-fed words

As pied and appled as your portmanteau,

As neat as your regards,

As Porlock as your heart.

Harvest Thanksgiving

So white, the days are sown
With lack and leat of corn,
    So bright, my blade has cut
    On waste and wheat.
With glut and need I till and turn,
With loss and load I stack the barn.

I work the brilliant trench
    That my joys store,
That my tears branch.
        In weather green or spare
        I wake the harrowing share
        Full with the husk and the ear.

Chervil and rye can spin
My fields alive with grain,
Barley and dock can burn
My various gold to corn.

Where leafs the oak, where falls the world,
My four months' purse is filled.
    I need no Sunday sight,
    For, look! my days are white.

The Boy with the Next-Door Face

The boy with the next-door face and the April ways
Who threw his hopes in the sky and walked the wall
With the sound of grass and the look of a hiding-place
Came when the hours grew tall
In the brushed and shining days.

On the spring of a four-leaved pride he raced and ran
Louder than rain on the dead and quicker than wind
That blows the six-foot man
Back to his window-pane
In the giant land.

Wild in the Indian spring he charged the lawn,
Wide in the cowboy summer he roped the field
Until the yew was old,
Until, on the stroke of doubt,
My camp-fire faiths went out,

My park pretensions called,
My supper reasons came,
And thoughts went hopping tame
Like birds at the crow of dawn.

Warm Pastoral

The still unravished bridegrooms press
The shutters of their quietness
   And foster-children snaps devise
   Their unremarked eternities.

The still unravished bridegrooms play
And bawl across the shouting bay
   While slow time runs beside the sea
   And rescues Rhyl from Arcady.

Heard music sounds along the sand
And sensual ears on every hand
   Give sensual lips the leaf-fringed lie,
   And lovers kiss, and springs go by.

The camera tries its marble tricks,
But from the snap the broad script speaks
   Unteased beyond the thought of Rhyl:
   "Us in the water. Em and Bill".

To Adonis, in January

Now having, Lycon, evolved the ancient truths,
    And having made a song of an old air,
Having formed a conviction, Aristus, like the old faiths,
    From despair, which is the old despair;

Having childed, Ceres, with the same old spring
    And lost my childhood, Koré, with the ancient doubts,
I come again to the old discovering
    Of the same new leaves that reward the same old shoots.

Having seen the same old branch grow gaunt in the sere,
    Having held the infant leaf in its second spell,
All I can tell you, Adonis, is that spring is near
    And the world is well.

Your Kiss, My Linnet

Your kiss, my linnet,
    Your arms that close
On the twofold minute
    Create our loss.

    And from your face
My preterite present peers
Grief deep in older years
    And ties my hands
    And knots my snare
And limes my grave
    That tried am for my wounds,
    Convicted of despair,
Condemned to love.

Under This Informing Sky

Under this informing sky
   I step, the cynosure of stars,
   The council of elected years
Claims me in its chancery
Lawed and ordered as the sea
   Beating on domestic shores.

Rule my judgment in my hand,
   Time my sentence by my hair,
   Tell me that the vanes may veer,
Tell me that the sails may stand;
Not the nonconformist wind
   But blows an edict everywhere.

Ground and shrouded, I am yet
   Centuried and seasoned by,
   Headcuffed in a gaol of day

Stay me hobbled, lay my plot;
Still an unaccustomed thought
Will slip out of the galaxy.

The Frock the
Spider Wears

The frock the spider wears
Is buttoned with her tears,
    Leaves from the gibbet fall
    To their own funeral.

The stream that sucks the sluice
Gulps out its loss,
    Winds of the year's disfavour
    Behead the lover.

The eye that spins distress
In the spider's dress
    And signs the leaf to doom
    In a winding tomb

Blows in a deathless way
The head's decay,
    Streams in a griefless weir
    The heart's despair.

The Garden

Piecefield the burrowed fosse,
Build with a bride's lace
The hemlock's house;
Make, as you mark,
The waygrass fall erect
Round the nettle architect
And the arable dock.

Watch. The ditch blazes, blows,
And all your yardspace loves
Thrive in your air,
Shoot in their sleeves!
This is the garden, is it not?
Where now you cultivate the root
As once you would in a farthing plot
With fingers too particular
Correct one curling rose.

The Black Sheep Returns

No long arm christed me. No crook
Savioured me, bleating, to the flock.
    Alone I launched the paths that failed
The cliffs that creviced to my walk
Where the barbed wool hangs black
    On the wire of the world.

The compass of my care,
    My trick alerted me
When that exploring needle star
    Which scouted me
Led to the north of God and skinned
The shearing wind.

The sun that sailed from my guilt
    Tempered my suit.
    Thoughts in the crossless night
      Fed me; the brand

No font contrived, no water named
Sang in my shank like salt.

Climbing the looking scar,
Vexed on the serry, tricked in the clefts,
I purchased the way's gifts,
Sniffed all the scarce and spin
Of the shuddering loin,
The fall from the stair
And the wreck
Of the handslipped stack.

Like him I licked the way,
Like him I picked the climb,
And all the widowing day
I heard the chime
Of trouble in an echoing joy,
Till on the bland and bell-less plain
Like him God's side slipped in,
Still spoiling for endeavour,
The lack and bedrock over,
To the domestic, peakless wold
Of that incomparable fold.

This Amaryllis Grass

This amaryllis grass
That cools me close
Swaths qualms and qualities

And the waned field
Where clouds and cares are pooled
Stacks the ricked world.

That pales and pours me in
This spotless green
Must stitch from sleep

The various buttercup
That for distinction's sake
Will catch me awake.

A Letter to Tiberius

The cuckoo greening on the April stair
   Looks for a branch to lay his tenant voice;
But you, Tiberius, have no need to cheer
   Your natural homelessness.

The urchin apple sucking in the sap
   Gropes through the wasp its ripe and ready grin;
But you, Tiberius, have no need to tap
   The summer through the sin.

From walls and orchards in your level land
   Brides on the lawns a happiness of snow;
A million widows weeping in the wind
   Made that one blaze to blow.

Night Hangs the Hone on the Hook

Night hangs the hone on the hook; the pail
Snores on the cobble; the sucked well
   Slaps in its cradle; cows breathe
   Milk, and the byre wind dreams through its teeth.

The drive and gravelled trudge of dark
Fades out of work; locks cluck; doors bark;
   The kettle rumours on the stone
   The bead and cowl of a tune.

Evening has mothed in wool and wing
The binder's bite and the scythe's sting
   That from her woman shade may nerve
   The crystal and cut of love.

Ankling in the Wade

Ankling in the wade
Of the shore sea's reach
Here I can broach my spade
And touch
For skulls a shell, for bones a bottle, drowned eyes
Green glass; driftstock and grape
For the ragged ship
And tumbled sailors for toys;
A fish of Tyrian weed
For the shoal of the sad,
Large wood for the long dead.

The mounted waters fathom
The pinnacle and plunge
Of sands and walls,
Works, days and pails
And toppling Troys of human

Shores; swell to a war,
Give for starfish a sponge,
For matchstick a nailed spar.

But out in the trained bows,
Up to his catch in the sound,
The salt-faced mariner knows
Nacre in the clam's rind,
Pearl in the sea's plunder
Milk in the carrion cray
Whirlstones as tinder
And in the roaring sky
A fire to stare his winters by.

Easter

Church fires on chestnuts shine
For autumn's bread and wine,
Transfiguring hands begin
Their evidence of green,
Stigma of violet stirs
The ghost from the grass.

So from the bone tree's burrow
My seed puts out tomorrow
And brows with fledge and spike
The wood and the wick
While from the root of rumour
My hares, like hopes, scut into summer.

Brighter than the bearded cloud
Hands of the brakes blade
The line of hope's cloth
And the key of a turning faith

Clocks in the cuckoo bough
Where all my falls shall blow,
Blood out of mind,
As salt in an old wind.

Sea, What Makes
You So Blue

Sea, what makes you so blue?
    Is it the day?
    Is it the sky
    From the coloured quay
To the wake's bow?

It is the fall
Of the stalling keel
    That once prowed by
Like launched gull.
It is the paint on the hull
And the blue sail.

Sea, what makes you so deep?
Is it the lap
    Of the heaped sand
    At the tack's end
    That shelves to the sound?

It is the weight
Of the drowned bait,
    Of ballast and bones
    In the coral dunes
And blood
In the amber weed.

Sea, what makes you so calm?
Is it the home
Of the bay's arm
To the travelling stream?
Is it the moon?

    It is the sleep
    Of a sail top,
Rest and room
Chapel and chime
    And the turn of space
    In a sailor's eyes.

Letter from a Dead Lover

Do you remember
   This hand you made that marched the paper
Down where the red woods wander
     Into verse?
     Your craft the course
   Of its keeper?

And all that night
   This catalyst, your need,
     Changed the night's form,
     Took you in your own arms,
Made you your lack, your light
   Litany and lord?

And have you memory
   Now that the covered grass,
     Bleak page and buried prayer

Testify

In what uncovered ways

How many deaths you are?

At Gwales

Long in the lovely room I stayed
    Stored with sap and synthesis,
    Being only the waves that lace
        The sunlight on the tamarisk
        And the slatted leaves that hide the husk,
Green and glad.

The wall broke in on the breaking water,
    The eyes blinked in dividing blood.
        Towards Aber Henfelen I saw,
Where the gales of Cornwall scour and scatter
        The paper leaves at the brain's door,
    The quick thorn in the virid wood.

The Dream-Hole
in the Wall

The dream-hole in the wall
    Enlights a tower or tomb
    Where sounds and voices come;
    Sometimes work's drum
Or love's footfall

Hangs, but above the tree
    That bars the measured gate,
    Old beyond dreams or doubt,
    Where battles and flags fought
Coil in heraldry,

Eyes to the slit spy
    Beyond the tinkling wars,
Gagged in the trumpet day,
    Chained in the sieging stars,
    The bird and breadthless gyres
Of the momentary sky.

The Apple Tree

My sleeves are worn
And the sage worm
Burrows his wits
At my brash roots,
My threadbare stem
Breaks the sour green,
My bent legs hold
The shape of the world.

Once was a woman
(The earth was new)
Came like dawn
To my kindling snow,
Stretched for the helpless gems of my hands
Where Alpha's knowledge sucked in my veins
And the slow worm slid on the bough.

My memory like my bark is thin
But wise as winter and flaunt as flame,
Old as Phoenicia, slight as sin,
She wept in the crook of my brain.

A pasture of springs in my workday wear
I laboured with my leaves for her
Dug for the sun with a curdling prayer
And with my boughs
Strove till the sinuous air was green,
Pushing the sap vows
Up through the well-used skin
To build her a house.

One day
She lay
Clenched in my shade,
Old as Phoenicia, white as a cloud.
My scalled stems played
A shadow's rune
And glad as God
I worked the loam and my tumbling spray
Hung with its summers round her womb.

With my scalled stem
I built a skein
Of leaves about her face,
Latched her with lace,
Called the first blackbird from the croft
To my sane arm's cleft,
Summoned the swallow
to match his minims at my green elbow;
In July
Flowered like a knight my white-mailed vair
To velvet her floor,
Rivalled the may
And with my green talk stroked the sky.

And then, one day,
She came with a child,
Old as Phoenicia, cold as the world,
And she has gone away.

The Fern in the Sun

The fern in the sun
Is the cryptogam.
   Frond and fibre rise
From humus and haulm,
The leaf and the loam
   Work their synthesis.

The fern in the shade
Is the spire of God,
   Esoteric, immune.
   And from this I discern
   The essence locked in the bloom,
The world in the word.

Afterword

The second child of a successful Latvian immigrant leather trader and his English wife, Rosamund Stanhope was born in Northampton in 1919, the same year that T.S. Eliot published his essay "Tradition and the Individual Talent" in *The Egoist* (and the same year that publication folded). Stanhope was trained as an actress at the Royal Central School of Speech and Drama, but with the outbreak of the Second World War, she joined the Women's Royal Naval Service (the "Wrens") as a radio mechanic and worked for the BBC. After the war ended, she served for a time as a secretary for Miron Grindea's *ADAM International Review*, and then she studied to be a schoolteacher, a job she held until her retirement in 1987. After the publication of *So I Looked Down to Camelot*, her first book, Stanhope concentrated for a while on writing novels, none of which have been published. But in 1990, Peterloo Poets published her second collection of poems, *Lapidary*, followed by a third, *No Place for the Maudlin Heart*, in 2001. As stalwart and ambitious as her poems—she suffered a broken spine in a fall in 1963, the same year she earned an external degree in English from the University of London, and was thereafter partially paralyzed and often hospitalized and in pain—she was also curious and adept, having once, according to her daughter Louise Larchbourne, taken her television apart and put it back together "just to see how it went."

So I Looked Down to Camelot was first published by John Rolph's Scorpion Press in 1962, one year after Roy Fisher's *City* (Migrant Press, 1961) and one year before Rosemary Tonks's *Notes on Cafés and Bedrooms* (Putnam, 1963), two formidable works of British poetry from the same time period that serve as examples of directions very different from the one in which Stanhope set out. Near the end of his aforementioned essay, Eliot writes of the "laudable aim" of "divert[ing] interest from the poet to the poetry," and while I'm about to do just that, I won't pretend to offer a "juster estimation" of Stanhope's poetry than those at which other readers might arrive. Moreover, while I don't wish to deprive anyone of the joy of discovering—both immediately and over time—the seemingly endless satisfactions and surprises in Stanhope's work, I think a brief and partial consideration of one poem might demonstrate those pleasures.

In his 1959 essay "Five Ways of Looking at a Tree"—first published in *The New Statesman*, in which Stanhope also published work—John Berger describes a tree from the points of view of a philosopher, a poet, a lover, a painter, and what would seem to be an engineer, although he never uses that word. "The engineer begins to measure and count; the lover luxuriates; the philosopher extrapolates . . . [t]he painter studies the sheer presence of colour and the angles of the boughs," writes Joshua Sperling in his recent book on Berger's life and work. But what does the poet do?

According to Berger, she closes her eyes "[i]dly and every so often," after which she sees the tree "imprinted on [her] retina" in a different color and compares the sunlight's strength to that of breaking waves, herself to "a small island . . . in the grass." She hears children playing nearby, and, "by some association too quick for [her] to notice," this leads the poet to note the impressive amount of birds that can be concealed in a tree, their eventual departure and return resembling "painted birds on a fan suddenly opened and then slowly shut again." "For [the poet], above all," Berger writes, "this tree exists in time, and its size and its greenness and the reasoning of the man who originally planted it, no less than the man who may order it to be felled, all remind [her] of this fact." Nowhere is this notion more palpable than in Rosamund Stanhope's "The Loud-Leaved Trees," a poem in which we find the speaker not only obsessing over an object's necessary existence in time, but doing so with an engineer's precision, a lover's relish, a philosopher's powers of induction, and a painter's ability—which is also a *desire*—to, in Berger's words, "sort out what [she] can see."

Like many of the poems in *So I Looked Down to Camelot*, "The Loud-Leaved Trees" consists of stanzas of uniform length and lines of irregular length. (The bulk of its lines consist of six or eight syllables, but some contain as few as two and others as many as ten.) Stanhope is a rhymer, though her patterning is never rote or static, and her complex, muscular sentences never allow her poems to devolve into doggerel or chant. The first stanza of "The Loud-Leaved Trees" teases us by both introducing rhyme and frustrating our expectations regarding its deployment. Three of the stanza's line endings —"trees," "dogmatise," and "images"—all end with z-sounds preceded by different vowel sounds, while "face" ends with a less buzzy s-sound that's more kith than kin to its fellow last words. Each line also contains an internal vowel rhyme—the long e's of "leaved" and "trees"; the long a's of "shape" and "face"; the short a's of "can" and "dogmatise"; and the short i's of "virid" and "images"—but we don't get a rhyme *scheme* until the second stanza, when a clear *abba* pattern is established.

This lasts until the last stanza, at which point the poem both exchanges its established pattern for another familiar one (*abab*) and reveals where its early turn ("But when the whisper of the year") has finally taken us; that is, when the

"Winter philosophies concede / What in the thought-shaped twigs the spider mends," the poem takes a different sonic shape. A new season, which was but a "whisper" in the summer, has now come to power by way of "Logic," "Concept," and "Abstraction." (These words are all placed at the beginnings of lines and so capitalized, thus allowing for adherence to poetic convention and to personification.) The concession is of course one season yielding to another, but this yielding is also a gain, for when the tree is stripped of its leaves, we see a new and different patterning, as the "[s]errate" and "entire" green of the "thought-shaped twigs" has revealed the "lace intelligence" of the spider who has made its home in them.

In an early section of his book *I and Thou* that begins "I contemplate a tree," the philosopher Martin Buber writes: "The tree is no impression, no play of my imagination, no aspect of a mood; it confronts me bodily and has to deal with me as I must deal with it—only differently." Walter Kaufmann, Buber's translator, notes in a footnote that "Er leibt mir gegenüber" ("it confronts me bodily") is, more literally, "it bodies—across from me or vis-à-vis me," and indeed Stanhope's flora are often "bodying," as her speakers encounter trees with "a summer face," a garden with "eyes," and corn wearing "gowns." But the poems themselves seem to "body" as well, as if I'm being confronted by someone with whom I must deal, which in turn reminds me that Stanhope is the only other poet that could have written Wallace Stevens's line "Take from the dresser of deal," though according to her daughter, Stanhope didn't read Stevens until the early 1990s, when she gave Stanhope his *Collected Poems*.

I mention this not only because Stevens's use of the word "deal" to mean cheap pine wood echoes Stanhope's predilection for words uncommon in poetry, although that's certainly true. (As Larchbourne wrote to me in an email, "I suspect that, as in the case of e.e. cummings, she tended to be reduced in the critical view to a characteristic—in this case, of using unusual vocabulary.") Rather, what's more pleasurable to me is the way that Stanhope's poems, like those of Stevens, often set up expectations that end up being deliciously and immediately undermined; or, to use Stevens's words, the way they "resist the intelligence / Almost successfully." For instance, when I read Stevens's "The Emperor of Ice Cream"—a poem I've surely read more times than I can count—I always briefly read "dresser" to mean "someone who is dressing," only to have that vision snatched away by the next line, which then reminds me that the word refers to furniture. I'd wager that it's Stevens's use of word "roller" in the poem's first line ("Call the roller of big cigars") and the three preceding appearances of the word "emperor" (which brings to mind nakedness) that juke me.

Similarly, the second stanza of "The Loud-Leaved Trees" contains a moment that never fails to thrillingly trip me up:

> *Using this green prerogative*
> *Of metaphor and may*
> *They have their integrated say*
> *Serrate as elm, entire as love.*

Here, the word "may" at first feels like the modal verb that signals wish or permission, making "may / They have their integrated say" feel, for a moment, like a request. But of course "may" here refers to hawthorn blossoms, which are named after the month in which they appear. To borrow from Stanhope, syntax eventually "invades the scar" of my misreading, but for a moment I experience something akin to what music critic Greil Marcus says happens when he listens to certain of his favorite records: "[E]ven though I can recall every note in isolation, know everything that is coming, the contingency you can hear . . . opens up the performances, so that, in a sense, when you listen, you don't know how the songs will turn out, and you're shocked every time at what happens."

One of my favorite aphorisms is Theodor Adorno's "Der Splitter in deinem Auge ist das beste Vergrößerungsglas" ("A splinter in your eye is the best magnifying glass"), and as is the case with many texts to which I return again and again,

I've given a good deal of thought to the circumstances that might have given rise to such a sentence. In a footnote in his book *Thought-Images: Frankfurt School Writers' Reflections from Damaged Life*, Gerhard Richter notes that Adorno might be riffing on a German proverb, "ein Brett vor dem Kopf haben" (literally, to have a piece of wood in front of one's head), that's used to describe someone who's slow on the uptake or block-headed, and this seems to me a reasonable conjecture. For my part, I've often tried to picture the gloomy Adorno writing *Minima Moralia*, the book in which his aphorism appears, in sunny Los Angeles, where he sought refuge from the Second World War, and have thought that maybe he had in mind the environmentalist pioneer John Muir, as it was Muir's accident at an Indianapolis wagon-wheel factory—an awl pierced the cornea of his right eye on March 6, 1867, which was also the day of a total solar eclipse—that precipitated his naturalist calling. (I wonder, too, what Adorno's friend Walter Benjamin—who, as Susan Sontag reminds us, loved "playful miniaturizations of reality as the winter world inside a glass globe that snows when it is shaken"—would have made of Stanhope's "Miniature Snowstorm.") But while both of these hypothetical origin stories are compelling to me, their confirmation would not increase my fondness for Adorno's sentence, which I'd argue is too curiously evocative, too satisfyingly oblique to be reduced to its origins.

So, too, are the poems in *So I Looked Down to Camelot*, which neither respond well (if at all) to guesswork regarding Stanhope's well-lived life nor are reducible to their at-once traditional and inimitable formal features. Here is a mind "[e]clectic in its work," a work that's both "wise as winter" and generous in its "orchard affluence." I'm so very glad to have this book back in the world.

GRAHAM FOUST